HAL•LEONARD®
CELLO PLAY-ALONG

AUDIO ACCESS INCLUDED

Wedding FAVORITES

VOL. 4

PLAYBACK+
Speed • Pitch • Balance • Loop

To access audio visit:
www.halleonard.com/mylibrary

Enter Code
7162-1387-4100-7460

ISBN 978-1-4950-7317-5

Trischa Loebl, Cello
Audio arrangements by Dan Maske
Recorded and Produced at Beat House Music, Milwaukee, Wisconsin

HAL•LEONARD®
7777 W. BLUEMOUND RD. P.O. BOX 13819 MILWAUKEE, WI 53213

Visit Hal Leonard Online at
www.halleonard.com

All I Ask of You

from THE PHANTOM OF THE OPERA

Music by Andrew Lloyd Webber
Lyrics by Charles Hart
Additional Lyrics by Richard Stilgoe

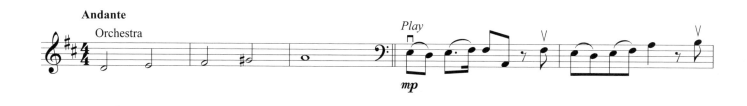

In My Life

Words and Music by John Lennon and Paul McCartney

Somewhere Out There

from AN AMERICAN TAIL

Music by Barry Mann and James Horner
Lyric by Cynthia Weil

Moderately, with expresson

Electric Piano

close 2nd

1st   close 2nd   close 2nd   3rd

4th f

mp

Electric Piano

Guitar solo

Highland Cathedral

By Michael Korb and Ulrich Roever

Sunrise, Sunset

from the Musical FIDDLER ON THE ROOF

Words by Sheldon Harnick
Music by Jerry Bock

molto rit.

a tempo

mp

rit.

A Time for Us
(Love Theme)

from the Paramount Picture ROMEO AND JULIET
Words by Larry Kusik and Eddie Snyder
Music by Nino Rota

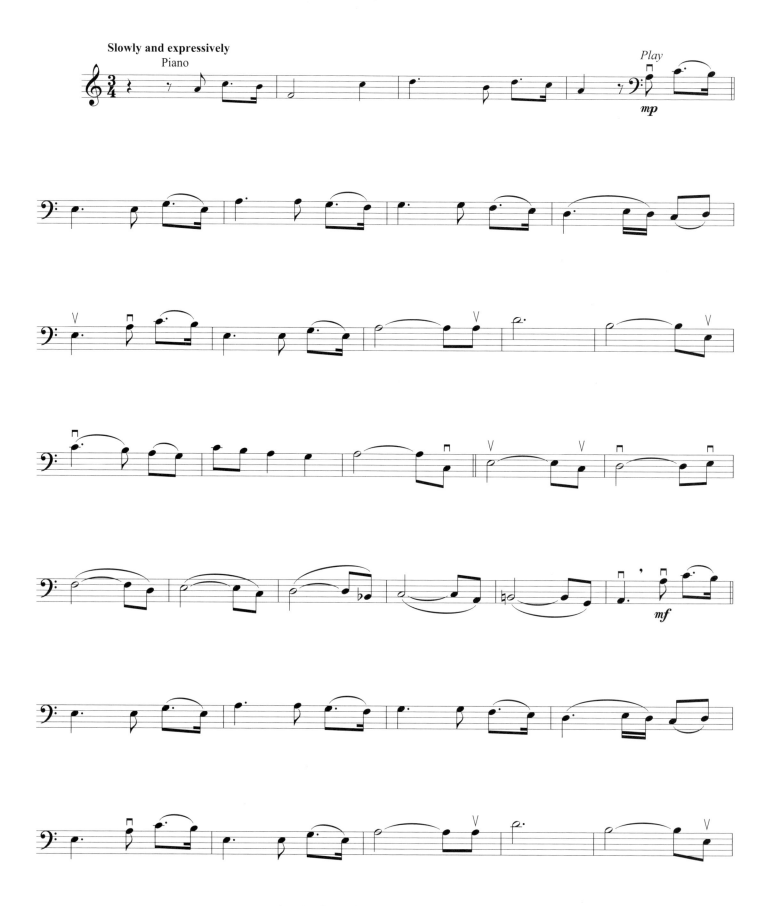

We've Only Just Begun

**Words and Music by Roger Nichols
and Paul Williams**

Wedding Processional

from THE SOUND OF MUSIC

Lyrics by Oscar Hammerstein II
Music by Richard Rodgers